Marla's Good Idea

by Rosa Lester   illustrated by Sean O'Neill

Scott Foresman
is an imprint of

PEARSON

Glenview, Illinois • Boston, Massachusetts • Chandler, Arizona
Upper Saddle River, New Jersey

Every effort has been made to secure permission and provide appropriate credit for photographic material. The publisher deeply regrets any omission and pledges to correct errors called to its attention in subsequent editions.

Unless otherwise acknowledged, all photographs are the property of Pearson.

Photo locations denoted as follows: Top (T), Center (C), Bottom (B), Left (L), Right (R), Background (Bkgd)

Illustrations by Sean O'Neill

ISBN 13: 978-0-328-50802-0
ISBN 10:　　0-328-50802-0

10 V010 15 14 13

Marla was bored. She went to her
big brothers' room to see if they wanted
to play with her.

"You can't come in," they said. "We
are trying to make something for the
science fair at our school."

"What will you invent?" Marla asked.

"We don't know yet. Please go away
so we can think," said her brother Mike.
"I can help you," Marla replied.
"No thank you," said her other
brother Dan. "You are not old enough.
You are just a little kid and your poor
ideas will mess things up."

"I have lots of good ideas," Marla said. "Please let me help."

"You need to find something else to do," answered Mike. "Look, you can have that piece of wire. Just go away and let us do our work."

Poor Marla. She was very unhappy. She almost started to cry. Instead, she got an idea.

I will make something of my own, she thought. I like bubbles. I like things that are sweet. I will make bubbles you can eat. I will reuse this piece of wire for the wand.

Marla thought about what she might need. She made a list and gave it to her mother. Her mother got everything on the list.

Then Marla measured and mixed. She sifted and stirred. She put in sugar and syrup and other sweet things.

Then, at last, the mixture was done. It was time to carry it into the yard and test it out.

Marla took the wire she had brought
from her brothers' room. She made
it into a bubble wand. She stuck the
bubble wand into the mixture.

Marla blew into the wand. A perfect
bubble flew in the air.

Marla caught the bubble on her
tongue and let it pop in her mouth. It
tasted wonderful.

Marla called her friends Jake and
Lucy. They came over to her house.

They blew bubbles and let them land
in their mouths. They danced around
catching them, laughing and making
noise.

Dan and Mike came outside to see
what was going on.

"You are not supposed to eat bubbles!" Dan said. "They will make you sick!"

"Not these," said Marla. "I made them special. Try them."

Marla blew a bubble at her brothers. Dan ate one. Mike ate one. Then they ate some more.

"Marla, you are most amazing," said Dan.

"These are yummy! You have given me an idea for the science fair. We can make a machine that blows different flavors of your bubbles at the same time," Mike said.

"Yes," said Dan. "Will you help us make it?"

Marla smiled. She said, "I think that is a great idea!"

A Cool Kid Invention

Read Together

Have you ever eaten a Popsicle™? Did you know that a kid invented them? It's true. Frank Epperson invented Popsicles when he was just 11 years old.

Frank liked to mix together different flavors of soda. He wanted to know how they would taste if they were frozen. So, one very cold day, he mixed some sodas together in a glass. He put the glass outside. The next morning the drink was frozen solid. The wooden stirring stick was still in it. He pulled the stick out. Out came the frozen drink. It tasted great, and that was the beginning of the Popsicle.